To:

_____

Your love has given me
great joy and encouragement.

PHILEMON 7

From:

_____

Faith, Hope, & Charity...Forever Friends

Written by Jody Houghton
with Doris Rikkers
Illustrated by Jody Houghton

inspirio
The gift group of Zondervan

Faith

Oh, hello there. My name's Faith.

My friends say that I'm always available when they need me most. You know, I'm the one they call when they've got the down-in-the-dumps blahs and they don't really know why, or they want to celebrate and need a friend to laugh with.

Très Jolie (pronounced Tray-ja-lee) here is my precious kitty. Her name means "pretty one" in French, but I just call her Très for short. She's a bit persnickety but I love her anyway. She's faithful to me and I to her, so we get along just fine. I always try to have a word of encouragement for my friends. My motto is "I know you can't see it yet but trust me, everything will turn out just fine." Oh, and while you're waiting, I just made brownies—have one, it'll make you feel better.

Faith

The only thing that counts
is faith expressing
itself through love.

GALATIANS 5:6

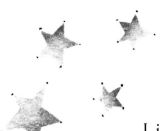

Little Things

It's just the little, homey things,
The unobtrusive, friendly things,
The "Won't-you-let-me-help-you" things
That make the pathway light.
The "Done-and-then-forgotten" things, ...
The "Laugh-with-me-it's-funny" things,
The "Never-mind-the-trouble" things,
That make our world seem bright.
For all the countless, famous things, ...
Can't match the little, human things,
Those "Oh-it's-simply-nothing" things,
That make us happy, quite.

EVA M. HINCKLEY

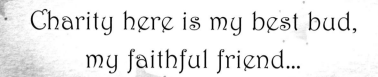

Charity here is my best bud,
my faithful friend...

I hear from her at least once a week by phone, or e-mail. Not only does she remember my birthday with the perfect card she shopped for all year but she sends me funny cards in between just to make me laugh. Last month when I had the flu she made me chicken soup (OK, it was from a box, but she took the time to be with me). Then we watched a sappy movie together. But what makes her so special is that she believes in me when I don't believe in myself. I treasure her friendship and I treasure her prayers.

Faith

A Friend Like You

When it's cloudy outside
I have sun in my day
Because of a friend like you.
When my purse holds no coin
I'm still richer than kings
Because of a friend like you.
Friends like you share the good times.
Friends like you share the tough times;
And all in-between times too.
And though I don't say it
As oft' as I should
I'm glad for a friend like you.

SARAH MICHAELS

A friend loves at all times.

PROVERBS 17:17

"It's a perfect day for golf," I said.

"The sun is shining, the temperature is warm and there is only a hint of a breeze rustling the trees."

"And it will be the perfect game, if we don't keep score," Charity commented.

"Oh, but we have to keep score!" Hope replied, "How else will we know if we got better than the last time?"

Charity tees up her first
ball, takes three practice swings
and she's ready. She adjusts her grip, her
hat, her feet one last time and swings –s-s-s.
It's a perfect swing. But there's no ping, no
crack, no contact.
The ball has
dribbled away
from the tee!
Simultaneously Charity and
I break down into fits of
laughter. We're always laughing about something –
it makes an ordinary
afternoon a delightful one.

Faith

Let love and faithfulness never leave you;
Bind them around your neck,
write them on the tablet of your heart.

PROVERBS 3:3

Tablet of my ♡

14

A true friend
shares freely,
advises justly,
assists readily,
adventures boldly,
takes all patiently,
defends courageously,
and continues a friend
unchangeably.

WILLIAM PENN

Hope

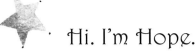

Hi. I'm Hope.

My friends always say that I'm there for them—
even when all else fails, there's always Hope.
I love getting up early in the morning. The dawn,
the first light of the new day brings such promise,
such hope for starting over and making a
difference in the world. Wow, just talking about
it gets me revved up! Even on cloudy mornings—
there's always the hope that the sun will come
out later. And mornings are the perfect time to
talk with God. Before I get too wrapped up in
all my other activities I feel closer to him.

Well, I should go. I need to water my African
violets and order the fruit kabobs for teatime.
Oh, do join Faith, Charity and me for
tea sometime, we must talk.

And remember, if you want something deep in
your heart, something that God wants too, and
expect it to happen—it will! God has promised us!

Hope

Those who bring sunshine
into the lives of others,
cannot keep it from themselves.

JAMES M. BARRIE

There is a joy that never ends
between the hearts
of faithful friends.

JODY HOUGHTON

Put your hope in the LORD
both now and forevermore.

PSALM 131:3

May the God of hope
fill you with all joy
and peace as you
trust in him.

ROMANS 15:13

"I love wearing hats!" Faith exclaimed.
"Wearing a hat makes me feel so sophisticated,
so special, so elegant. Hats make me feel good."
"I know," Charity agreed. "I love hats with flowers,
feathers or beads. I wear hats in the garden
and hats to church. The world would be
happier if we all wore hats. They're so fun,
they make you happy."
"Oh, I agree completely," I chimed in. "I always
say that hats make the woman—they're the
crowning touch to any outfit. They're the
exclamation point at the end of a strong
statement. Our hats say who we are.
And mine has FUN written all over it!"

Hope

The blessing of the LORD
be upon you;
We bless you in the
name of the LORD.

PSALM 129:8

Of all the lovely treasures
At the rainbow's brilliant end,
One brings lasting pleasure:
A dear and trusted friend.

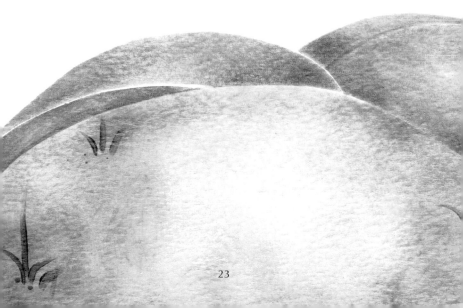

There's nothing like a relaxing day at the beach with friends...

well, perhaps three or four days at the beach is even better, but we always take what we can get. Sitting on the beach is cheap therapy: the sun warms our bones, calms our brains and soothes our nerves. We smother our bodies with lotion and let the sun soak up our worries.

The last time we were at the beach Faith spotted a slim girl in one of those itsy-bitsy bathing suits. "Were either of you ever that thin?" she asked. "I don't recall ever having a body like THAT and now gravity has set in and ... well .... Can you help me get out of this chair?" "Never mind," I told her.

"Looks don't really matter, anyway. It's what's inside that counts. And besides, God loves us just the way we are, big hips and all."

"Oh, stop worrying about it," Hope said. "Just be happy you can stand the sun. Where's the sun-block? Put up the umbrella! If I stand out here in the sun much longer I'll look like a spotted lobster!"

As we settled in for the afternoon of reading, talking and laughing, I silently thanked God for the blessings of sun, warmth, friends and fun.

Charity

There is a friend
who sticks closer
than a brother.

PROVERBS 18:24

Oh, the comfort, the inexpressible comfort
of feeling safe with a person,
having neither to weigh thoughts,
nor measure words,
but pouring them all right out—
just as they are,
chaff and grain together—
certain that a faithful hand
will take and sift them ...
keep what is worth keeping ...
and with the breath of kindness
blow the rest away.
DINAH MARIA MULOCK CRAIK

27

Charity

Good
Thoughts
Grow
Into Love

You know, I am so glad to meet you.
My friends have told me about you.

Friends are so fun! They make you laugh. They
let you cry—but not for too long (crying does
terrible things to your eyes, you know) and then
they help you laugh again: at yourself, at your
circumstances, at whatever is wrong. I love that
about faithful friends. But, oh, forgive me, I forgot
... (I do that a lot lately). Let me introduce myself.
I'm Charity. And, well ... I just love everyone! I can
usually spot the best in anyone after three minutes of conversation. There's something to love
about everybody—even if it's only their smooth
elbows, a nice smile or pretty toe nails.

I always say if you look for the good in
anybody you can grow it into love. I've even
made this plaque to remind me. And I use that
quote a lot on the handmade gifts I make for
my special friends. It's my own little
way of spreading love around!

Charity

It is right for me to
feel this way about ... you,
since I have you in my heart.

PHILIPPIANS 1:7

Love one another deeply,
from the heart.

1 PETER 1:22

A true friend is the gift of God,
and only he who made
hearts can unite them.

ROBERT SOUTH

I'm the baker in the bunch.

I love to bake and then invite my friends over to eat my latest cakes, cookies or brownies. Baking is an adventure for me. I love mixing things together to create delicious smells and delectable delights that thrill your taste buds. Oh, I know, everyone worries about the calories, but trust me, I always bake things that have something nutritious in them.

Like my Best-ever Apple Cake is just loaded with apples. And besides you wouldn't want me to not bake and waste one of my God-given talents, would you?

My Nutty-Fruity Cookies are so-o good for you too. They have cereal, oatmeal, nuts and raisins in them. And if I'm inspired I throw in a dash of wheat germ! Coco thinks my cookies are the best—don't you, Coco? Well, I must get back to baking—the girls are coming for tea this afternoon.

Faith

You, my friend,
are the rainbow of my life:
the pastel, the bright;
the pot of gold;
the promise after the storm;
the reminder that
God loves me.

CONOVER

For the LORD your God
will bless you ... in all the
work of your hands and
your joy will be complete.

DEUTERONOMY 16:15

Simplify, simplify, simplify—
that's my latest motto.

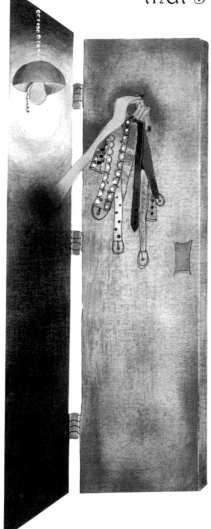

So in a moment of high energy I had the focus and vision to clean up and clear out, starting with the closets. Hope came over to help and was amazed at what I had accumulated in just a few short years. (Okay, it's really been ten years since I sorted and tossed.)

"How can you have all these belts and nothing to go with them? What ARE you saving them for?" she called from the closet.

"I don't know. I just couldn't decide what to do with them—they're still all so good."

"But these are two sizes too small for you. Get rid of them!" she added emphatically.

And so we continued to pitch, among other things, twenty-two slightly smashed gift bows, one pointed-toe-yellow-high-heeled shoe that matched the sun dress I outgrew three years ago, twenty-three cleaner bags, 101 extra hangers, and five faded collectibles from far away places.

Cleaning the closet makes me feel so-o-o good—like I've accomplished something that will last forever. And you know, work shared with friends doesn't seem like work at all—especially if you have a good laugh while doing it.

Charity

Two are better than one,
because they have a
good return for their work.
If one falls down,
his friend can help him up.

ECCLESIASTES 4:9-10

My Friend

Who always shares a sunny smile?
Sits and visits for a while?
Walks with me that extra mile?
My friend does.
Who lets me know I'm understood?
Never speaks a word that's rude?
Does things helpful, kind and good?
My friend does.
Who's this friend who cares for me?
Helps and comforts willingly?
Mirrors Christ in all I see?
Y—O—U!

SARAH MICHAELS

Like most animal lovers, we love our pets.

We think they are the most special creatures in the world. I have a cat named Très. Her favorite pastime is watching dust particles dance in the sunbeams as they shine through the skylight window. She thinks she's a princess and we don't have the heart to tell her otherwise.

Coco is Charity's little dog. He's a brown poodle mix and is eager to please her or anyone else for that matter. He loves to help, especially when Charity cleans out the refrigerator! His tail wags incessantly no matter what he's doing. Hope, with her allergies and all, has settled

40

for a darling little canary named Buttercup. She is a bright, sunny yellow. When the sun shines Buttercup sings and twitters all day long. When it's dismal and gray, she still sings and twitters all day long! We feel that our pets are just another way that God tells us, "I love you!"

Faith

How many are your works,
O LORD!
In wisdom you
made them all;
the earth is full of
your creatures.

PSALM 104:24

The Best Treasure

There are veins in the hills
where jewels hide,
And gold lies buried deep;
There are harbor-towns where the
great ships ride,
And fame and fortune sleep;
But land and sea though
we tireless rove,
And follow each trail to the end,
Whatever the wealth of our
treasure-trove,
The best we shall find is a friend.

JOHN J. MOMENT

Faith and Charity and I can laugh and giggle about almost anything until our stomachs hurt and tears stream down our faces. I often have to remind Faith to calm down because she can just scream with delight over something. I'll never forget the time I put purple hair spray in my hair for my birthday. We still laugh when we recall the crazy looks and reactions we got from people. And the other day we laughed at Charity because she responded to our comments with a phrase that came straight from her mother's mouth. We have all vowed to each other that we would never turn into our mothers ... now that we seem to be doing it anyway we can't help but laugh hysterically about it!

Hope

A friend is someone who shares with
you a smile, a tear, a hand.
A friend is someone who cares for
you; a heart that understands.
A friend is someone you can be with
when there's nothing to do.
A friend is someone you can laugh
with—I'm so glad that friend is you.

CONOVER

God has brought me laughter.

GENESIS 21:6

The third Saturday of every month my friends and I gather for morning coffee...

This is always a great time for us to catch up on what we've been doing and plan our next outing together. Just last week, Faith showed up with brochures from a travel agent.

"I thought we needed to go some place different—someplace exotic," Faith explained. "So I stopped by the travel agent and picked up these brochures."

"Oh-h-h, an adventure! That sounds fun. Hey, look. We could spend Christmas in Israel and see Bethlehem," I said. "Or how about this one?— kayaking down the Amazon!"

"No way." said Hope. "That's a bit too exotic for me—I'd probably break out in a rash from the high humidity. And I don't even want to think about the bugs ... the snakes ... the ...."

"Okay, forget that. Here's one. Safe but adventurous," said Faith. "'Cruise the Nile in the comforts of home on our luxurious cruise liner. See the Pyramids, the Sphinx, the blowing and drifting sands of the Sahara. Go back in time to the greatest civilization that once was. As you sail, dine on shrimp buffets and enjoy top-notch entertainment,'" she read to us.

"Sounds good to me," we all said together laughing. "Move over Cleopatra, here we come!"

Charity

The LORD bless you
and keep you;
The LORD make his face shine upon
you and be gracious to you;
The LORD turn his face toward you
and give you peace.

NUMBERS 6:24–26

Lord, help my friend to glimpse
the rainbow through the tears,
to see your light shining
in the darkest night,
and to behold your love
reflected in me.
May your love be with her
wherever she goes.
Amen

I think it's so important for friends to stay connected—

by phone, fax, real mail or e-mail. I just love e-mail.
Don't you? I mean, it's such a great way to stay in
touch with everyone. Just a few tap-tap-
taps on my computer and presto—I've
sent a cherry message
instantly to a whole
bunch of friends.
E-mail is chatty.
It's informal.

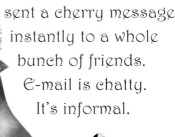

It's like talking on the phone but you can edit your words before you send it. When I talk on the phone my mouth goes faster than my brain and I end up saying the silliest things! But with e-mail I review what I've said before I send it—it's great. Oh, did I say that already? I forget—I often do that, you know, and then I don't remember what I was originally going to say—oh well. Where was I? Now I remember—staying in touch. My friends appreciate hearing from me, even if it's about the little everyday things. Sending little messages to let them know I'm thinking about them is what matters. And knowing "you've got mail" adds an exciting moment to everyone's day.

Charity

Every day I pray for God
to bless you as you have
blessed me, my friend.
And I thank him for your gift of
friendship's shared joys and sorrows.
You are in my heart, my thoughts, my
prayers ... you are my friend.

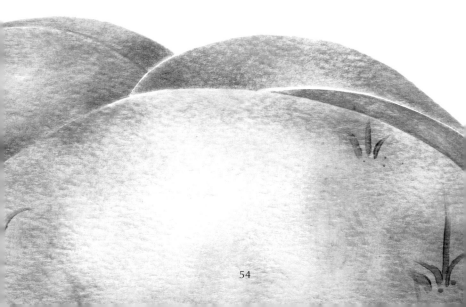

The LORD your God is with you,
he is mighty to save.
He will take great delight in you,
he will quiet you with his love,
he will rejoice over you with singing.

ZEPHANIAH 3:17

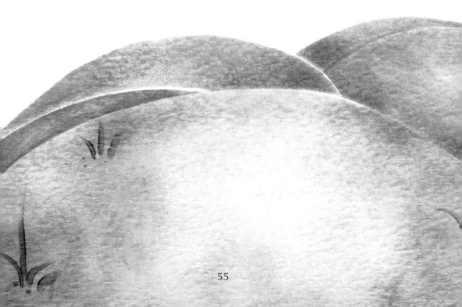

Everybody loves a bargain and my friends and I are no exception.

"Shop 'til we drop"

Faith

Bargains Galore

50¢

SALE

Sidewalk sales, garage sales, bargain basements and dollar stores give us the thrill of getting a deal. Whenever we see the sign "Closeout," or "50% off," our pulses race and our spines tingle as we dig through piles of sheets, housewares, jewelry or gift wrap with great vigor. We eagerly await our semi annual bus excursions to distant outlet malls when we stock up on wedding presents, bath accessories, shoes, designer paper plates with matching napkins, and replacement pieces of our Christmas china. At the end of the day we happily brag about how much money we saved with little regard for how much we actually spent!

Hope

May God give you
the desire of your heart
and make all your
plans succeed.

PSALM 20:4

A friend is a present
you give yourself.

ROBERT LOUIS STEVENSON

Do everything in love.

1 CORINTHIANS 16.14

Day Spa

There's no better way to pamper yourself than with a day at the spa...

even if the spa happens to be in your friend's bathroom. Charity, Hope and I love to beautify ourselves every once in a while with hot mud masks and deep-root hair treatments. We manicure our nails, purify our pores and rub our elbows and knees with luxurious imported lavender cream. Once we even tried that new hot rock massage therapy after we saw it on a morning talk show. We have no problem finding new ways to relax. Now, if we could only find a cream that would dissolve inches from our hips!

Faith

You always let me blow off steam
And don't condemn me for it.
And when I've made a huge mistake
You kindly will ignore it.
You let me be just who I am
Right now, this very day.
God bless you, my special friend.
I'm glad you came my way.

CONOVER

A cheerful heart
is good medicine.

PROVERBS 17:22

Every time the phone rings I pick it up with anticipation,

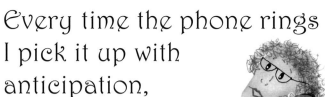

hoping it is a worthwhile call from a friend rather than a worthless opportunity to change my phone service—again. Talking to Faith or Hope on the phone is the highlight of my day. When talking to them I can allow my mind to spill out of my mouth— I can say how I really feel about what happened in my day: the highlights, the harrowing, the annoying. When others wouldn't have a clue about what I'm talking about, my dear friends do—sometimes they even know how I feel at my first hello.

And by the end of our conversation, I feel much better. They have reassured me that God is good and today's problems will pass. But above all I love the way they always close our conversation with a cheery "God bless."

Charity

My friend is one who
speaks to me
and takes the time to write;
Who has a thought to spare for me
whatever day or night;
The one who knows the faults I have,
but does not criticize,
And who is always at my side
to help and sympathize.
My friend is one who keeps me in
her constant memory,
And now and then will turn to God
and say a prayer for me.

DON DUPUY

Let us love one another,
for love comes from God.

1 JOHN 4:7

Above all, love
each other deeply,
because love covers
over a multitude of sins.

1 PETER 4:8

Several weeks ago my friends and I gathered in Faith's garden

to admire her flowers when Charity exclaimed, "Oh, Faith, what beautiful daisies! Those are daisies, right?"

"Those? No, those are Black-Eyed Susans. Daisies are yellow in the middle with white petals. These have black eyes and yellow petals," Faith explained.

"Oh," said Charity. "White petals, yellow petals, they all look alike to me. I guess I'll never keep all

the names of these plants straight. I'll tell you what, you can talk to them and call them by name. I'll just tell them how pretty they are and that I love them all!"

We all love flowers, even if they make me sneeze. Being in the garden, surrounded by flowers, brings us a little closer to God.

Whether our hands are in the dirt or our eyes are watching a butterfly dance on the purple coneflowers, we feel his presence around us.

Hope

The Best Treasure

There's happiness in little things,
There's joy in passing pleasure.
But friendships are,
from year to year,
The best of all life's treasure.

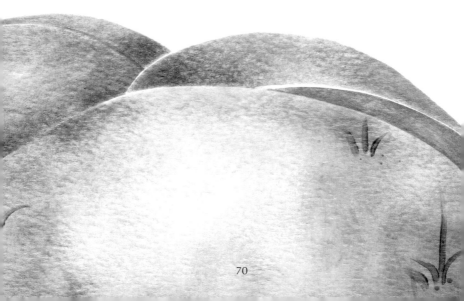

A flower cannot blossom
without sunshine,
Nor a friendship
without compassion.

JODY HOUGHTON

A friend is one who knows who you
are and gently invites you to grow.

JODY HOUGHTON

When I feel overwhelmed by the problems of the world, I head for the tub. There is no more peaceful place than a bathtub filled with hot water and a gazillion bubbles. It's calming and quiet and

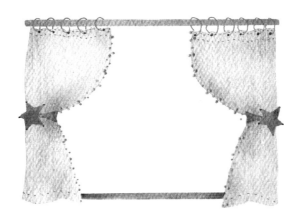

I'm all alone with my thoughts and my little yellow rubber ducky. I let the answering machine get the phone calls, I turn down the lights, light a candle or two, find a favorite magazine and ease myself down into the white bubbly foam. The warm water soaks away my physical aches and my mental pains. Sometimes the warm bubbles help me think clearly, at other times they let me daydream. It's all so relaxing and quiet and peaceful: a perfect time to meditate and talk to God.

Charity

Perfume and incense
bring joy to the heart,
and the pleasantness
of one's friend springs
from his earnest counsel.

PROVERBS 27:9

Did You Know

Did you know you were brave,
did you know you were strong?
Did you know there was one leaning hard?
Did you know that I waited
and listened and prayed,
and was cheered by your simplest word?
Did you know that I longed
for that smile on your face,
for the sound of your voice ringing true?
Did you know I grew stronger and better
because I have merely been friends with you?

"You know it's so great that we get together like this for tea,"

I said. "Charity, I love your new dress—that purple looks great on you!"

"Thanks. Your hat is just adorable. Is it new?"

"No, I just bought some purple peacock feathers and added them to this sun hat I had. I think it makes it so cheery."

"Teatime makes me feel so alive, so young. Being with friends and dressing up makes me feel like I don't have a care in the world," Faith said.

"Oh, I know what you mean," agreed Charity. "Relaxing with friends, eating divine foods and sipping tea is close to paradise. By the way, what kind of tea is this?"

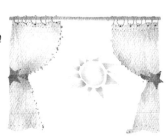

"It's a special orange peel blend that I discovered at the gourmet tea shop," I answered. "I thought you'd like it. It goes perfectly with Faith's lemon bundt cake."

"Who brought these bite-size, chocolate-covered, caramel brownies? They're so cute ... and so-o-o good," Faith raved.

"I did," said Charity quietly.

"Did you make them?"

"Well ... not exactly—my friend Sara Lee helped me out!"

Hope

The Miracle of Friendship

There's a miracle called friendship
That dwells within the heart,
And you don't know how it happens
Or when it gets its start.
But the happiness it brings you
Always gives a special lift,
And you realize that friendship
Is life's most precious gift.

I thank my God every time
I remember you.
In all my prayers for ... you,
I always pray with joy.

PHILIPPIANS 1:3-4

Several years ago Charity came up with the idea that we should all go birdwatching.

"Birds are birds—they're all alike," Faith had complained.

"Oh, but birds are the paintbrushes of the sky that add motion to the picture of life," Charity had poetically retorted.

And so we went off into the woods looking for the little specs of flight that we needed to identify in a split second or less.

Birdwatching is interesting for us but a bit of a challenge. Any time that I have to stay perfectly quiet and not comment or laugh or make any noise at all is the ultimate test of my self-control. Hope keeps a meticulous listing of every sight, sound and species we happen to see. She has a list of what, where, and when we spotted our first chickadee! We all had a riotous laugh when Charity insisted that she had spotted the elusive Pearlescent Breasted Robin.

Birdwatching is a good test to check out a friend. If you can all be comfortable with each other even in total silence—well, that's special.

Charity insists that birdwatching is good for us all. It reminds us that God is in the little things. If he watches over even the birds of the air and protects them—surely he will then watch over birdwatchers like us!

Faith

Thank You, Friend

I know I've never told you
In the hurried rush of days
How much your friendship helps me
In a thousand little ways;
But you've played such a part
In all I do or try to be,
I want to tell you thank you
For being friends with me.

May the LORD show
kindness to you,
as you have
shown ... to me.

RUTH 1:8

Love yourself:

✔ Take a hot bath with lots of bubbles.

✔ Read an entertaining novel.

✔ Dream of a week at the beach with friends.

✔ Write down your daydreams.

✔ Take a catnap (even if you don't have a cat).

✔ Name at least ten blessings God has given you.

✔ Claim fifteen minutes of solitude in your garden.

✔ Watch your favorite video for the seventh time.

✔ Pick or buy some flowers for yourself.

✔ Make yourself a cup of tea.

For in loving yourself
you'll be better at loving others.
("Love your neighbor as yourself." Galatians 5:14)

Charity

May kindness and
faithfulness be with you.

2 SAMUEL 15:20

He who clasps the hand of a friend
holds tight to a blessing.

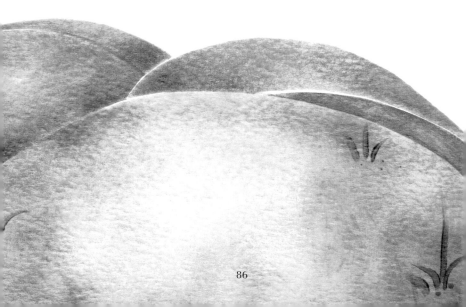

Life has no blessing
like a caring friend.

It brings comfort to have friends in
whatever happens.

SAINT JOHN CHRYSOSTOM

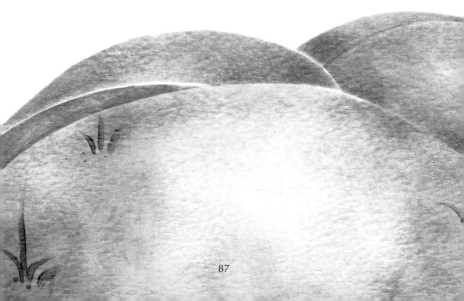

There was a time when we had visions of obtaining and maintaining perfect bodies.

You know, musical aerobics, major workouts that worked up a sweat. But we quit doing pushups when all we could think about were pushup ice cream pops. Curl ups for the stomach gave us visions of cream curls sprinkled with powdered sugar. And squat thrusts only made us want to thrust our hands into the nearest bag of chips.

Now we just stick to walking around the mall to give our hearts a bit of a workout. And if we're good we reward ourselves with a cup of coffee. If we're not so good we stop for a cinnamon roll—one of those gargantuan ones covered with white, gooey icing and containing a month's worth of fat grams.

Either way we feel exceptionally righteous that we actually took the time to exercise!

Hope

Dear friend,
I pray that you may
enjoy good health
and that all may go
well with you.

3 JOHN 2

Friendship is a chain of gold
Shaped in God's all perfect mold.
Each link a smile, a laugh, a tear,
A grip of the hand, a word of cheer.
Steadfast as the ages roll
Binding closer soul to soul;
No matter how far or heavy the load
Sweet is the journey
on friendship's road.

"It's a perfectly lovely day,"

I said over the phone to Charity. "Let's all go on a picnic. Call Hope and tell her to scrape up some- thing from the frig and the cabinet. We'll go potluck and see what we come up with."

"Great idea," Charity agreed. "Let's meet at Riverview Park in an hour."

As my Faithful Friends and I gathered at the park we couldn't wait to share what we had chosen for our surprise lunch. "I brought the vegetable," I announced. "I brought fruit," chimed in Hope. "This will work out great," said Charity, " 'cause I brought the cheese."

The three of us dove into our baskets and pulled out our goodies. One look at our food choices and we all burst out laughing. I had brought carrots – in a carrot cake. Hope's fruit was strawberries covered in chocolate sauce and powdered sugar. And Charity's cheese was a creamy caramel-covered cheesecake.

"This is the best picnic we've ever had!" Hope laughed. "Great minds think alike!"

Faith

You will go out in joy
and be led forth in peace;
the mountains and hills
will burst into song before you,
and all the trees of the field
will clap their hands.

ISAIAH 55:12

Friendship is a
sweet responsibility.

JODY HOUGHTON

The joy that you give to others is the joy that comes back to you.

JOHN GREENLEAF WHITTIER

I pray that you will receive
double the joy you
have given to me!